SCHOLASTIC News

Nonfiction Readers®

D0377848

Let's Vote on It!

By Janice Behrens

Children's Press®
An Imprint of Scholastic Inc.
New York Toronto London Auckland Sydney
Mexico City New Delhi Hong Kong
Danbury, Connecticut

These content vocabulary word builders are for grades 1–2.

Subject Consultant: Eli J. Lesser, MA, Director of Education, National Constitution Center, Philadelphia, Pennsylvania

Reading Consultant: Cecilia Minden-Cupp, PhD, Early Literacy Consultant and Author, Chapel Hill, North Carolina

Photographs © 2010: iStockphoto: 5 inset (Steve Goodwin), 5 inset (Eric Isselee); All other photographs ©Ken Karp.

Art Direction, Production, and Digital Imaging: Scholastic Classroom Magazines

Library of Congress Cataloging-in-Publication Data

Behrens, Janice, 1972-
Let's vote on it! / Janice Behrens.
    p. cm. – (Scholastic news nonfiction readers)
Includes bibliographical references and index.
ISBN 13: 978-0-531-21346-9 (lib. bdg.) 978-0-531-21445-9 (pbk.)
ISBN 10: 0-531-21346-3 (lib. bdg.) 0-531-21445-1 (pbk.)
1. Voting–United States–Juvenile literature. 2. Elections–United States–Juvenile literature. I. Title. II. Series.
JK1978.B45 2009   324.60973–dc22 2009006373

8 9 10 R 18 17 16 15

CONTENTS

Vote for a Class Pet

We are getting a class pet!

We can get a goldfish or a hermit crab. How can we choose?

We will take a **vote**!

vote

Which pet should we choose?

First, we read books about goldfish. We read about hermit crabs, too.

We talk about what we like and do not like about each pet. That helps us choose which pet we want.

Goldfish

...e like

...around all day

...pretty animals.

...fun to watch,
...ly when you feed them!

Things we don't like

You can't pick them up or touch them

They like to hide in plants.

Their tanks need to be cleaned a lot

Hermit Crabs

...we like

...hold them in your hand.
...mb things and

Things we don't like

They might pinch you

BALLOT Box

VOTE HERE

We make a chart about goldfish and hermit crabs before we vote.

Time to Choose

Now we are ready to vote! Everyone gets a **ballot**. A ballot shows your choices when you vote.

We each color our choice on the ballot. Which pet would you choose?

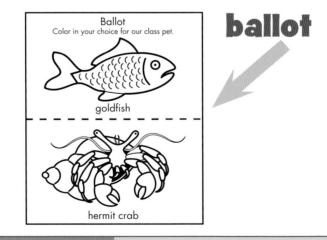

Ballot
Color in your choice for our class pet.

goldfish

hermit crab

ballot

Next, we fold our ballots. Then, we put them in a **ballot box**.

Our teacher says we do not have to tell anyone how we vote.

ballot box

We take turns putting our ballots in the box.

Which Pet Wins?

Finally our teacher counts the votes. She makes a **tally** to keep count.

The pet with the most votes will win! Which pet do you think will be the winner?

tally

ЖЖ //

Goldfish: III
Hermit Cra[b]: I

It's time to count the votes!

The goldfish wins! More kids voted for the goldfish.

Some of us voted for the hermit crab. That's OK! We will get to vote again. Soon we will vote for a name for the goldfish.

15

Let's Keep Voting

Voting is a fair way for a **group** to make a choice. You can even vote with your friends!

Which game would you vote for, kickball or jump rope?

group

Who wants to play kickball at recess? Who wants to jump rope?

Adults vote, too. In the United States, adults vote to choose our **leaders**.

When you grow up, you can vote to **elect**, or choose, our leaders. Until then, you can vote for kickball!

leaders

MY MOM VOTES!

Adults vote for our leaders. My mom lets me go with her when she votes.

1. We vote at a polling place. A polling place can be a school, library, or other place in your neighborhood.

2. We wait in line for our turn.

3. Mom goes into a voting booth. Inside, she pulls a lever to vote. She chooses the people she thinks will do the best job.

4. I know who my mom voted for. But I won't tell! Her vote is a secret.

YOUR NEW WORDS

ballot (**bal**-uht) a piece of paper that gives the choices in a secret vote

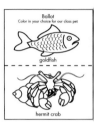

ballot box (**bal**-uht boks) a box with a slit on top to put votes in

elect (i-**lekt**) to choose by voting

group (groop) a number of people who work together or share something

leaders (**lee**-durz) people in charge who make decisions, like Presidents of the United States

tally (**tal**-ee) a count or a score

vote (voht) a way of making a decision where everyone offers a choice and the most popular choice wins

INDEX

FIND OUT MORE

Book:

Christelow, Eileen. *Vote!* New York: Clarion Books, 2008.

Website:

The Democracy Project: PBS Kids
http://pbskids.org/democracy/vote

MEET THE AUTHOR

Janice Behrens is a writer and Scholastic editor. She lives in Brooklyn, New York, with her family.